Shipping Homes

Beginners guide to building your own container home for a low cost

Includes plans and designs

By Jim Barris

Copyright © 2017

Cover photo courtesy of trybuild.org.au

Table of Contents

Introduction

Chapter 1: Traditional Shipping Container Usage 1

Chapter 2: Which Container is Right for You? 8

Chapter 3: Buying the Home of Your Dreams on a Budget 16

Chapter 4: Logistics - Transporting Your Shipping Container 21

Chapter 5: Location, Location, Location 24

Chapter 6: How to Protect Your Home Against the Elements 29

Chapter 7: Ways to Decorate Your Shipping Container Home 36

Chapter 8: How to Give Your Home an Addition 41

Chapter 9: Providing Maintenance for Your Container 44

Resources 47

Conclusion 48

Other books by this Author 49

Introduction

This book covers all you need to know about building your own shipping container home, even if you are a beginner to the subject.

At the completion of this book you will know what process to follow in order to build your own shipping container home, or if you lack the necessary skills what you will need to get done for you.

Once again, thanks for buying this book, I hope you find it to be helpful!

Chapter 1: Traditional Shipping Container Usage

It's not far-fetched to admit that converting a shipping container into a living space is a bit unconventional. But hey, with tiny homes becoming increasingly popular all over the world, it's no surprise that the rectangular, house-like shape of a shipping container has attracted people to buying them and transforming them into beautiful, untraditional homes.

While shipping containers still are mostly used for carrying cargo back and forth large distances overseas, a complete history of the shipping container is needed so that you as a potential shipping container homeowner can be knowledgeable about the past and present uses of the shipping container.

This chapter will focus on much more than history. It will also detail the typical dimensions of the most popular shipping containers that are used in naval transport as well as outline the different types of shipping containers that are available for purchase.

Having this information is the first step in figuring out what you want your specific container home to look like.

Shipping Containers, a Brief History

While it may seem like shipping containers today have a wide variety of uses, they were originally designed to carry a large number of goods overseas. It's easy to take this type of cargo transportation for granted. In fact, shipping containers have been an integral part of how people transport goods for centuries.

The shipping container as we know it today would not exist if it weren't for an innovative gentleman by the name of Malcom McLean. McLean began working in the transportation industry in the 1950s, using ground methods with trucks as his primary source of good transport.

His business was actually the fifth largest trucking transportation business in America at one point. While McLean's business was certainly doing well, he became frustrated by the increasing number of weight limitations and taxes that were being added to his ground cargo. McLean witnessed the process of loading and unloading cargo from his trucks taking multiple hours. As he became more and more tired of the heavy fees that were bogging down his business, his mind continued to ponder how he could change the logistics industry. At the time, he had no idea that he would come to revolutionize it.

Eventually, McLean came to the conclusion that in order for a more standardized form of shipping to be possible, he would need to design a new method of how goods were carried. Foregoing his lucrative trucking business in 1955, he sold it and took out a bank loan for roughly forty-two million dollars. Instead of sticking with the road, McLean headed to the sea, and used seven million dollars of his money to purchase an existing shipping company.

He then set his mind to designing a state-of-the art shipping container, one that would be lockable, easily loadable and unloadable, stackable, and strong. His ultimate design is how we know the shipping container today. What's more, McClean was able to offer his customers a 25% discount compared to his competitors, because his methods of shipping were standardized and significantly cheaper.

In 1957, McClean took his first voyage from New Jersey to Miami on the first cargo ship that was designed to carry his standardized containers. It turned out that he only needed to hire two dock laborers to load and unload his cargo. These men were able to move this cargo at an incredible rate of thirty tons per hour. This was unheard of at the time. By April of 1966, McClean's company was able to sail from the United States to the Netherlands with two-hundred and thirty-six shipping containers on board. This was no small feat.

Standardized Dimensions

At the time, McClean's shipping containers were thirty-three feet instead of the twenty and forty-foot containers that are standard in the cargo industry today. While the overall dimension for these two types of shipping containers differ, they also differ in terms of how people use them to their maximum capacity.

Of course, it's safe to say that you're not reading this book with the intention of using a shipping container to actually transport goods, but both the twenty and forty-foot shipping container can offer advantages and disadvantages depending on their use. While there are many different types of shipping containers that are available for purchase, the two basic dimensions that are offered are twenty and forty feet.

Dimensions of the 20 Ft. Shipping Container

	Length	Width	Height
Internal	19 Feet, 2 Inches	7 Feet, 8 Inches	7 Feet, 9 Inches
External	19 Feet, 10 Inches	8 Feet	8 Feet, 6 Inches
Door Dimensions	N/A	7 Feet, 8 Inches	7 Feet, 5 Inches

Additional dimensions that are important for the twenty-foot storage container include:

- **Internal Area:** 144 sq ft. (13.38 sq m.)

- **Weight:** 4,840 Pounds (2.2 tonne)

Dimensions of the 40 Ft. Shipping Container

	Length	Width	Height
Internal	39 Feet, 5 Inches	7 Feet, 8 Inches	7 Feet, 9 Inches
External	40 Feet	8 Feet	8 Feet, 6 Inches
Door Dimensions	N/A	7 Feet, 8 Inches	7 Feet, 5 Inches

Additional dimensions that are important for the forty-foot storage container include:

- **Internal Area:** 300 sq. ft. (27.87 sq. m.)

- **Weight:** 3,800 Pounds (1.72 tonne)

It's important to note that there are also high cube containers available, which add an additional foot to the shipping container. For the forty-foot unit, this means that instead of the container offering 6 feet of height on the inside after insulation, it will offer 7 feet. This might be a desirable option for the taller container homeowner.

Advantages and Disadvantages between the 20 Ft. and 40 Ft. Container Options

From the tables above, it's easy to see the advantages and disadvantages that exist in these two-dimensional types in the simple terms of size; however, there are additional details that are important to note. For example, while the twenty-foot shipping container is easier to transport, it's overall square footage is more expensive than the forty-foot container option. While the overall price for the forty-foot container is more expensive than the twenty-foot storage container, the price per square foot is higher.

Due to these reasons, the forty-foot shipping container has been consistently the more popular option, for both people who want to transport goods and for people who are looking to convert a shipping container into something more practical.

The forty-foot option is generally seen as being the one that offers "more bang for your buck", and the amount of square footage on the inside of the shipping unit is considerable, especially when compared to the twenty-foot unit.

Types of Shipping Container to Consider

While the dimensions of various shipping containers are fairly consistent in the sense that there are only one of two options from which to choose, the type of shipping container that you can purchase offers much more potential variety.

Here we will look at specific types of shipping containers that you might be interested in eventually purchasing. While descriptions will be available for each option, the pictures that are included in this section will show you exactly what each shipping container looks like. Remember, these options can be ordered in either the forty-foot or twenty-foot dimensions.

Option 1: Dry Storage Container

If we transition from thinking about the storage container as something that carries cargo and rather look at it as a living space, this container offers a large front door option. The walls on each side can be customized to include windows. In terms of container options, this can be considered the classic style.

Option 2: Open Top Container

The open top container offers both the large front doors as well as the potential for a windowed roof. It seems like this container is asking for the creative mind to turn it into a spectacular living space.

Option 3: Tunnel Container

The tunnel container offers little in terms of privacy. With the two doors opening on either side of the container, it would be fairly easy to look inside. Of course, if you live in a secluded area, this might not be an issue.

Option 4: Double Doors Container

The double doors container offers much window space and scenic viewing. It would even be possible to put window glass over the length of the storage container and use the doors as planter space to make your garden more aesthetically pleasing.

These are just a few examples of the shipping container options that are available to choose from. The other ones that are available are more specific and not quite suitable for habitable use, such as thermal containers and car containers. The four options presented in this chapter should be able to give you an idea of what is available to you as you consider buying a shipping container for yourself.

Chapter 2: Which Container is Right for You?

Chapter one made it obvious that there are many decisions for you to make when deciding which shipping container to buy. Now that you have an understanding of the dimensions that shipping containers are comprised of, the next step is to decide whether or not you will go through with buying one. This chapter will document the pros and cons of owning a container home, and then will offer floor plans for how to pick a layout.

Advantages to Owning a Container Home

1. **Eco-Friendly**: Many people ultimately decide to build a container home because of the "green" nature of it. Thousands of steel containers are thrown away across the globe, and if you can save a landfill from having to bear the burden of one, more power to you.

2. **Cost-Effective:** The cost-effective alternative that shipping container homes offer make them a popular choice. They are also the perfect shape to be converted into a home. Sometimes, shipping containers can be obtained for free, making them much easier to own than a house that always has a price tag attached.

3. **Construction Ease:** If you were to opt to have all of your shipping container or containers pre-cut ahead of time, it would be possible for you to assemble your home in a couple of days. This is definitely an advantage for the construction-illiterate homeowner.

Disadvantages to Owning a Container Home

1. **The Challenges of Insulation and Heat Control:** Shipping containers are essentially large and enclosed steel rectangles. This means that they are prone to absorbing heat in the summer and absorbing cold in the winter.

While this can be solved with the proper insulation, insulation gives you less space inside your home. Additionally, if you look to AC units to satisfy your quench for cool in the summer, the eco-friendly aspects of the shipping container home become less significant.

2. **Rust:** If you opt to purchase a used shipping container home, know that your home might be closer to the end of its life span than you think. Shipping containers are prone to rust quickly, so if you buy a shipping container that is dented or scratched because you think that this gives it more of a "manufactured" look, know that it's likely your home will rust over time.

3. **Potential Health Risks:** Just as a reminder, shipping containers were not originally intended to be homes. It's possible that harmful substances exist within the architecture of the container such as lead paint, chromate and phosphorous. Long term exposure to these toxins can be deadly.

As is evident when listing the pros and cons of whether or not it's worth it to own a container home, there are arguments for both why you should and shouldn't invest in one. It's up to you as an informed consumer to decide what factors you care about, and invest time researching both the good and the bad aspects.

Now that the pros and cons have been defined, let's look at how you can design the layout of your container home, based on floorplans and pictures that people have designed in the past.

Keeping it Simple:

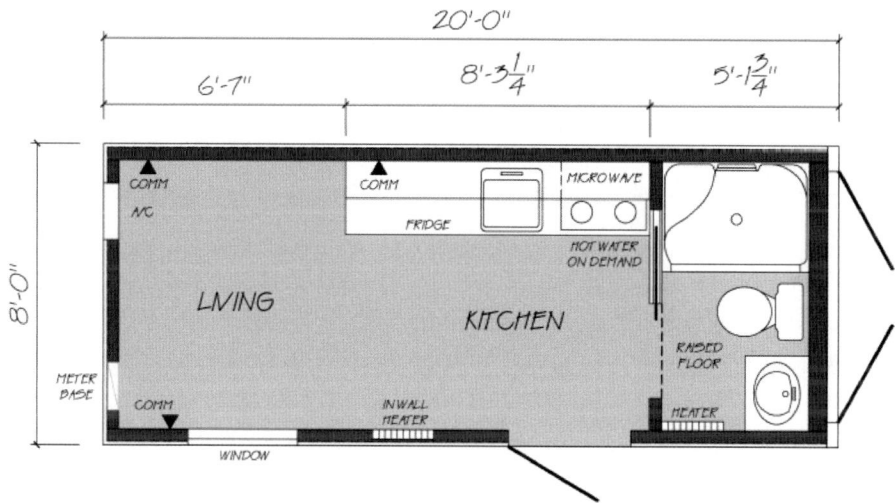

The first floor plan presented above shows a simple layout for a twenty-foot home. As you can see, the traditional doors that were originally used to gain access to the shipping container have been replaced with a wall so that there is room to build a bathroom. The biggest area of the house is the kitchen; however, the bathroom and the living room area only differ by about 1 foot. Additionally, the living area is also being used as the bedroom, making this floor plan the studio apartment of storage containers. It's safe to say that this particularly-sized container home might be best suited for someone living the single life.

Little Bit More Length

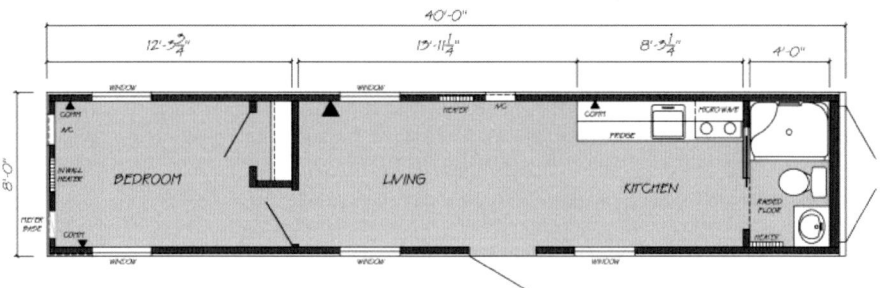

This floor plan is still a one bedroom, but reflects the dimensions of a larger, forty-foot container. It's important to note why the bathroom is in the same space as the previous floor plan. Because the bathroom is most likely going to be the smallest room in the house, there will be less square footage to properly insulate in that area.

The fact that the original shipping container doors open in that particular location makes the space near it a bit draftier. Also, notice that while in the previous floor plan the bathroom and the living room area were similar in size, the forty-foot plan offers a bedroom as well as a living area. This plan overall is significantly more spacious.

Floorplans with Multiple Bedrooms

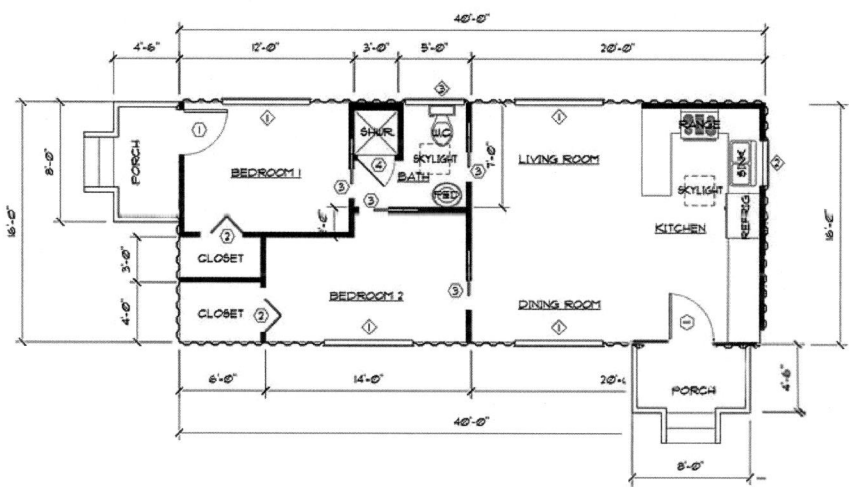

The last floor plan that we'll take a look at involves multiple bedroom units. As you can see, the storage unit used in this example is forty-feet long. The porches that are available at two separate areas of the house allows the two dwellers of this unit to enter the house via their own entrances; however, in order for the person who resides in bedroom 1 to get to the kitchen, dining room, and living room, he or she must pass through bedroom 2. Another interesting aspect of this particular floor plan is that it offers two skylights, one in the bathroom and one above the kitchen area.

These floor plans can give you a more accessible view of the different ways that you can plan your container's layout. Now we will look at some pictures of actual shipping container homes, to provide you with a proper overall visual.

Picture 1: Porch Access

An example of the porch in the last floor plan, this photo offers a view of a container's front porch capabilities. The pillars holding the porch up are similar to the style of the industrial-looking theme that the shipping container portrays in its entirety.

Picture 2: Stackable

Even though this diagram does not depict an actual house, it still sheds light on the stackable capability of a container home. By stacking three containers on top of one another, a multi-story home becomes possible. The circular windows additionally provide a unique twist to the space. Make sure that you have the proper zoning permits before pursuing this method of construction.

Exploring all Possibilities

This final photo seeks to show you the possibilities that exist by owning a shipping container home. While this home is exceptionally well crafted, one element of it that should be emphasized is the large bay window. By exposing one area of the home to natural light, the entire abode seems to look bigger. You should keep this in mind as you explore how to design your own container house.

Chapter 3: Buying the Home of Your Dreams on a Budget

While the pictures in the previous chapter may have made you feel like you want a container home immediately, it's time to talk business. This chapter will focus on the cost of a container home, with and without various options that you can either choose to indulge in or do without. Depending on your budget and style, you'll be able to get a better idea about how much certain designer choices cost along with the technical skills that you'll need if you choose to build the home yourself instead of hiring a contractor or professional.

Brass Tacks – The Cost of Materials

As was previously stated, it's possible to obtain a used shipping container for free; however, this isn't advised. If you buy a used one, you won't know how long it's been in use, and there's potential for it to deteriorate quicker than you may think. Here is a price breakdown of how much it costs on average for each step of your container construction process. For all of these categories, there is a range of costs because depending on how extravagant your taste and how large your budget, shipping container homes can get pretty fancy.

Material	Cost Breakdown
20 Foot Container	Between $1,400 to $2,800
40 Foot Container	Between $3,500 to $4,500
Flooring	Between $3,000 to $12,000
Glass Installation	Between $2,000 to $4,000
Heating and Air Conditioning	Between $3,000 to $7,000
Plumbing	Between $3,000 to $7,000
Electrical	Between $3,000 to $7,000

Roofing	Between $3,000 to $5,000
Insulation	Between $4,500 to $5,500
Site Preparation (Housing Foundation)	Between $8,000 to $14,000

Based on these numbers, let's say for example that you decide to go the cheapest route in terms of building materials and construction costs. You buy a twenty-foot container for $1,400, and from there you simply add up the costs for each additional category. This would bring your total to around $36,000. Other aspects of your home that you have to think about are whether or not you are going to hire a contractor to help you with special building skills that are necessary for this type of project.

The cost of a contractor starts at around $50 per hour and ends around $150. Obviously if you hire a contractor, there is great potential that this will increase the overall cost of your container home. Additionally, an aspect of the home that people sometimes overlook is laying the foundation. While laying the foundation has negative environmental consequences, it also costs a significant amount of money. Unless you're skilled in this particular industry, it's advised that you hire someone to do this for you. As you move forward in designing and creating your container home, remember to shop around for the best price.

Going the Prefabricated Route

The option also exists for you to buy a pre-fabricated shipping container home. While the overall price of these will run you anywhere from a mere $15,000 to a whopping $215,000, this type of home might be beneficial to you, especially if your handy skills are subpar. If you are interested in a prefabricated shipping container home, there are three main companies that sell them:

1. **Logical Homes:** Logical Homes designs your entire home for you. In a way, this company can be seen as an architectural

firm because they handle all the design, engineering, and all other necessary work before you receive your home. Below is a simulated photo of a container built by Logical Homes.

2. **Meka:** For more of a Scandinavian feel, check out Meka. This company's container homes look like they could be found in an Ikea store. Meka manufacture their products in the United States, so getting a container shipped to your location is a pretty straightforward process.

3. **Nova Deko Modular Home Solutions:** Based out of Australia, this company offers a wide variety of container homes that fit multiple types of budgets. The one below is available for $44,000.

While the advantages to purchasing a prefabricated shipping container home include less work, the reality is that once you start tacking on all the specifications that you want the prefabricated company to include in your shipping container home, costs can increase quickly; however, if you have the funds available this is certainly easier than building the home yourself. Also, if you know that you want a container home that is simple and quick so that you can live in it as soon as possible, the basic options that are included will keep your budget in check.

Make sure that when you discuss your options with a company that offers prefabricated homes, you bring up the topic of whether or not laying the foundation for your home is included in the price. As we saw in the chart above in this chapter, the foundation is one of the more expensive line items that are associated with building a container home.

Skills You Need to Build Your Home

If you are still undecided about whether you should buy your home prefabricated or build it yourself, here are some skills that you need to have in order to build a top notch shipping container:

1. **Design Skills**: Before you take hammer to nail, you need to have an idea of how you are going to design your home. A great tool that can help you do this is Google SketchUp. Find a design you like, and map it out using this application. You will need to plan measurements and sketch a tentative plan.

2. **Engineering Skills:** If you are planning to remove portions of the walls of the container and replace them with other types of materials, you will need to know how to properly reinforce the home so that it remains structurally sound. While minor cuts such as putting in a window might not call for much other than knowing how to cut steel, larger cuts may require some planning beforehand. Using an angle grinder to accomplish these cuts might be the way to go.

3. **Welding Skills:** You need to know how to tack weld, and depending on how exactly you want your windows to look, you may need to look into arc welding as well. Without having welding skills, you won't be able to make your windows, doors, and additional fixtures meet your aesthetic preferences.

4. **Working with Concrete:** If you are planning on building your own foundation, you need to make sure that the area where you're putting down your subfloor is level before you begin so that you don't run into problems while laying down your floor.

It's safe to say that this list is just the beginning set of skills you'll need in order to make a container home yourself. If you are looking at this list thinking that you might not possess all of the skills required, strongly consider hiring architects, contractors, and engineers, or purchase a prefabricated home. While it might be more expensive, it's sure to save you a headache or two.

Chapter 4: Let's Talk Logistics, Transporting Your Shipping Container

After you have purchased your shipping container, the next step is to establish how it will be sent to wherever you would like to build. This can be a stressful part of the process, and many current homeowners wish they had known more about it before creating their own. There are many factors to consider here: where the container is being delivered from, siting charges, insurance, what company is going to handle the delivery, etc. Some of the choices you have made in picking the container itself are going to influence the transportation, but it is good to know all of your options for getting the shipping container onto your property.

Where your shipping container is being sent from has a substantial impact on the delivery cost and timeframe. Most used containers will have been bought locally, and can simply be put on a truck and driven to your location. Delivery companies will typically charge a rate per mile, with prices averaging $2-6/mile for a standard twenty-foot container.

Note that the size of the container being shipped will have an impact on the overall cost of the delivery. Forty-foot containers are typically around 80-90% more expensive to ship than their twenty-foot counterparts. The type of truck being used to make the delivery is also important to establish. If you have the means to unload the container yourself, through the use of a crane or special forklift, then a standard flatbed truck is sufficient. If not, then a tilt bed truck is necessary to slide the container off the truck wherever it needs to be placed.

If the foundation is within easy access of the delivery truck, assuming it is a tilt bed, the truck can simply slide the container right on to its foundation. This is by far the easiest method of siting. If the location is not easily accessible, then you may need to rent a crane or an HIAB loader to lift the container off of the truck and drop it onto its foundation. However, be aware that the cost of renting the equipment to unload the container can be quite steep; cranes and HIAB loaders can cost several hundred dollars per day to rent.

If a brand new shipping container was purchased, it was most likely manufactured in Asia, and will need to be shipped overseas. There are two options to handle this; have the container delivered empty, or allow the container you bought to be used for cargo while it gets to your nearest port. The first option ensures that your container will be completely untouched when it gets to port, however you will have to pay the full delivery fee for shipping it across the ocean, which can cost several thousands of dollars.

The far cheaper option is to allow the container to be used as freight. The freight company will pay the delivery charge to have their goods shipped within the container, and then you will simply handle the delivery of the container from the port to your property. This is known as a one-trip, where the container is used to make a single delivery of goods before being transferred to a third-party owner.

The process becomes very similar to the local shipment that was just discussed, since you are not expected to handle the logistics of the container getting to port. You will just have to communicate with the freight company to establish when to expect the shipment to be fulfilled. If you live near a large international port, you can count on your container arriving in a short amount of time since deliveries will be quite frequent. It is highly recommended to purchase the container and arrange for the delivery from a single company, as there is much less hassle involved than dealing with multiple companies. Companies like J.B. Hunt and Shipped.com are convenient options for domestically transported shipping containers.

If you purchased a container abroad, then you will have to employ a freight company such as Maersk Line to handle the delivery. If you happen to have a commercial driver's license, then you may elect to move the containers yourself. Renting the necessary automobile and doing your own legwork is far cheaper than hiring a logistics company, however this is usually not a viable option for most people. The time in which you can expect your container to arrive depends on whether it is being delivered locally or internationally. Local suppliers can typically have your container on site within a week or two, however the international route could take months.

Insuring your containers may be another thing to include in your plan and cost estimates. Many large freight companies will include insurance within their transportation fees, but some consider it an optional upgrade. It is a good idea to question how much your containers are worth before deciding to insure them for delivery. For example, one to three used containers from a local supplier are usually not worth the extra cost of insurance. However, several brand new containers being shipped overseas for several thousand per unit are definitely worth the extra investment. A lot can happen on a 30+ day journey from China to New York, and it is certainly better to be cautious.

Chapter 5: Location, Location, Location

Any new housing development brings forth several questions about zoning laws, building permits, tax codes, etc. Unfortunately, there is no concretely established system for building a shipping container home in this country. As we have discussed, a shipping container home offers some advantages over a traditional house. However, since it is such a new and developing trend, regulatory bodies haven't quite worked out a way to handle it yet. There is no consensus for how to properly conduct inspections of such houses. In addition, regulation of permits is handled at the county or township level, and as such there is no single approach that is applicable to all cases. Research is required within the township you would like to build before taking any serious steps towards building a shipping container home.

Obviously, you must own a plot of land to build on before getting any kind of permit. With this kind of specialized housing, it helps to do some research before establishing where to erect one. Some areas may not be friendly towards this type of building since it is unclear how it may affect property values. More remote locales may be more accepting than suburban or city environments in this regard. Warmer climates with firmer soil (southwestern U.S. and dryer parts of South America, for example) seem to be the hotbeds for this developing trend, since it is easier to build the foundation and insulation isn't as much of an issue. The governing bodies in these areas seem to be more familiar and accepting of shipping container homes. The next step towards getting a permit to build is to draft all of the plans for your project to present to the local public works building department. Scaled blueprints, foundation plans, and project specifications are necessary to acquire a building permit in nearly all cases. Next, speak to the local authorities about these plans. Make any adjustments the jurisdiction requires to get your building up to code before formally applying.

It is important to make sure you have every necessary permit and thoroughly researched all of the local planning laws before starting any of the physical construction work. There are many horror stories out there of people who have had to tear down new construction projects after they failed to adhere to building regulations. Expect this to be a tedious process; the application alone can take up to a month to be reviewed, and permits can easily cost over $1000. More time and money will be necessary if additions or changes to the scope of work need to be made.

A particularly stressful part of the construction process is the inspection, as any homeowner can attest. Part of building regulation is routine inspections conducted by an official from the municipality. This is done to make sure everything is being performed in accordance to the permit that was granted to the project. Several inspections will need to be scheduled over the course of building your container home. The first is usually done before any of the concrete foundation is poured, called the footing inspection, to make sure the soil and any reinforcing rods will provide a solid base for the new building. The next inspection follows the completion of the foundation. The rest of the schedule will vary depending on the local regulations, but you may require a few more as your project progresses; usually after the insulation and ventilation systems are in place, and then again after the basic utility structures have been implemented.

Lastly, you will have a final inspection once the project is completely done to wrap things up. Some projects may require multiple inspections at the same stage if things are not up to code, which will stall your progress and can be quite frustrating, so it is important to be as thorough as possible and take every precaution when building. Though a tiresome process, it is a necessary one, since not only are you required by law to adhere to these rules, you want to make sure that your new home upholds all the standards of safety and security that have been established.

Since questions regarding the foundation of your container home will impact where you choose to build, let's discuss how to build one. The most common types of foundations built for shipping container homes are concrete piers, and slab-on-grade. Concrete piers are easily the simplest to make, and are little more than concrete cubes supported by steel rebar. A pier is laid for each corner of the container, and two for the center.

This type of foundation is great for allowing extra ventilation since the container rests off the ground. Slab-on-grade, or a raft, is more common for softer soil types, and involves digging a trench for the concrete to be poured into. It is recommended to work with a qualified builder or geotechnical engineer to make sure you are using the proper foundation and concrete type for what the specifications of your home require.

Examples of concrete piers, and slab-on-grade foundations

Normally, the weight of the container itself is enough to hold it in place on its foundation. It is common practice however, to either weld or bolt the containers into the foundation itself. Steel plates are placed at the corners of where the container will lay, before the concrete sets, and the container is welded to the plates at these points. If welding isn't an option you would like to go with, you can also simply drill through the bottom corner fittings and apply a 1" x 12" bolt here. Shipping containers are strong enough to only require fastening at the four bottom corners. If you are connecting multiple containers together, you should spray foam insulation into any connecting seams before either welding or bolting them together.

Here is an example of shipping containers welded into their foundations and to each other. Note the application of spray foam insulation in between the containers prior to welding in the third image.

Chapter 6: How to Protect Your Home Against the Elements

So you've got the container onto your property, and it's securely fastened into its foundation. There is still a lot to be done before it can be habitable. Perhaps the most crucial of which is properly insulating it. A house is meant to shield you from the elements, after all, and without insulation you will basically be living in a tin can; well, steel can. The way you insulate your new home is intrinsically tied to the climate the house is in. Cold, wet climates demand much more out of the insulation to keep the house warm and condensation-free; while hot and dry climates do not need to be as stoutly protected, and ventilation is more of a requirement. There are several types of insulation to consider, all on a cost-to-effect curve, with varying levels of installation difficulty.

Spray foam has proven to be some of the most effective insulating material money can buy. It not only provides a peerless R-value (a measure of the ability to resist heat flow), it also prevents corrosion and mold by providing a continuous vapor barrier. In addition, it is the quickest to install, can be applied to the interior and exterior walls, and its consistency allows it to adhere to nearly any surface and fit into gaps of any size. The only real downsides to using foam are the cost (estimated in price per board foot, a single shipping container would cost roughly $850 to insulate) and the mess; being an aerosol-foam, it requires protective gear to apply, and overspray is quite common to have to clean up.

Fiberglass insulation is the most common type, and is a more user-friendly and economical option than foam. Available in either blanket or rolled form, this material requires stud walls before installation. This type is good for most purposes, but you will need to install some form of vapor barrier since this does not protect much against condensation; overall a good option for warmer climates where not much insulation is necessary.

Insulation paneling is another option that is easy to install, with a high R-value for its density. This also requires stud walls prior to installation, and comes in pre-fitted sections to accommodate the spaces between your studs. Slightly more expensive than blanket fiberglass, paneling is a good option when you want to keep the thickness of your insulation down while still providing a high R-value, and don't have the budget for spray foam.

Spray foam insulation on the inside and outside walls of a container home

Fiberglass blanket insulation installed between wood studs; roughed-in electrical circuitry also shown here

Ventilation goes hand-in-hand with insulation when preparing your shipping container home. A properly ventilated home can be kept cool when needed, and defend against condensation that contributes to mold and rust. Simple vents are a common method of passive ventilation implemented in most container homes. Placed up high and at opposite sides of the container, vents provide a cross-flow of air through the unit by the power of the wind.

For homes that are settled on concrete piers or otherwise raised foundations, it is wise to incorporate vents into the foundation or crawlspaces to prevent condensation buildup, and increase heat flow through your floors. This works particularly well in cold environments. Turbine vents, or "whirlybird" vents, are also very effective at drawing air out of the container, and are very affordable for their utility (average cost of a good quality turbine is about $50). Placed on the roof of the container, these can be installed in minutes, and should only require maintenance once every few years.

Example of a louvered vent and whirlybird turbines attached to a shipping container

Active mechanical ventilation may be necessary in warmer climates where the passive systems need to be supplemented to keep the house cool. Many container homes implement extractor fans, an exhaust-only system, to draw warm air and humidity out. These should be placed as high as possible and furthest away from your largest source of air, usually a door or window.

In contrast, supply-only ventilation systems actively push air into the unit from the outside. This can be as simple as installing an air conditioning unit on the side of your container. A single standard 12,000 BTU Heat/AC unit is sufficient to keep even a forty-foot container nice and cool.

An exhaust-only extractor fan, and a supply-only Heat/AC unit installed on a container

Installing utilities into your shipping container home is not unlike any other conventional home. Along with the structural layout of the container, plans for the electrical and plumbing layouts should be drawn up before you start working on the house. You should know where you want your appliances and outlets to be placed before you frame out the inside of the container. Have an ideal location for the fuse box and the hook-up to the power grid in mind.

Mark locations on the stud walls for where the outlets and appliance hook-ups will be, and attach all electrical boxes to the studs before installing any drywall. Drill holes through the studs where appropriate and thread Romex electrical wiring through these holes to wherever they need to be; trying to be as efficient as possible. Most shipping containers have holes near the base to allow a forklift easy access. These holes can be used to house portions of your circuit if necessary. Chases for the plumbing should be drilled out of the floors and walls before insulating. The following is an example layout for an electrical plan, as well as an image of roughed-in electrical and plumbing systems.

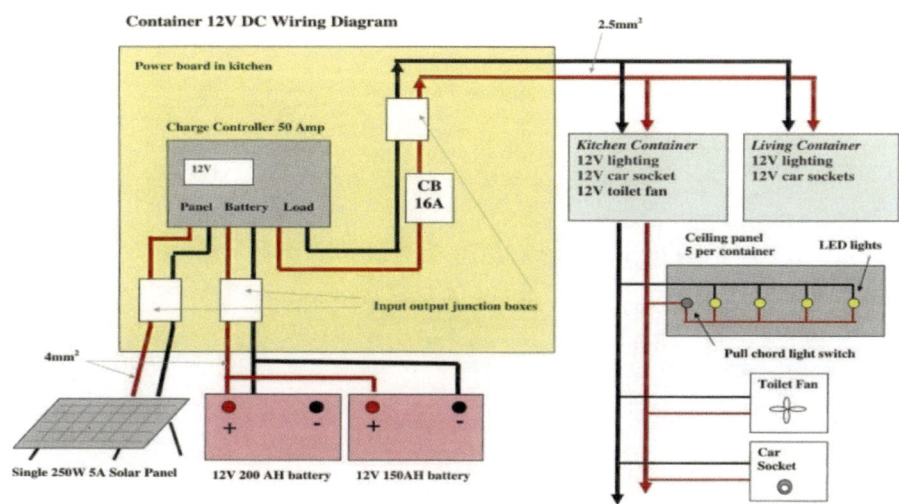

Chapter 7: Ways to Decorate Your Shipping Container Home

While shipping container homes can be considered to be quite unconventional, interior design options for your home might be equally as obscure. This chapter will focus on ways that you can uniquely decorate the inside of your home in way that will accentuate its overall design. Before you begin buying stuff with which to decorate your new and exciting home, it might be helpful to consider an overall theme that will contribute to the general feeling of the living space as a whole. Additionally, this chapter will give you great tips on how to save space, something that every smart shipping container homeowner should strive to achieve. To make these concepts easier for you to access, photos will accompany each design recommendation.

Interior Design Option 1: Curtains

Many shipping container homes are highly reliant on curtains. Because of how dark a container home would be without windows, big and expansive ones are often a staple of a well-designed home. This being the case, curtains are almost a must for a shipping container home. The picture below is a great example of how to maximize the use of curtains. These curtains enclose both the porch and the windows inside the home simultaneously, so that both the porch and the windows can be obscured at the same time.

Interior Design Option 2: Reflective Glass

While this option should technically be considered "exterior", reflective glass for your windows is another great option if curtains are simply not your thing. Opting for reflective glass allows you to forego the use of curtains so that you can see out even though no one can see in. Privacy is important, even if you live in a rather secluded area. Reflective glass should definitely be considered if your shipping container home is located where you are subjected to great views on a daily basis.

Interior Design Option 3: Stacking Rooms

Another way to design the tight space on the inside of your container home is to stack rooms or beds. In the picture to the right, you can see that the sleeping area is beneath the living room or television watching area. Attached to the base of the living room area is a rod with a thick dark curtain on it so that the bed can be isolated from the living room and surrounding kitchen area. Of course, it might be a bit hard to sleep if someone is watching television as you're getting ready to go to bed, but when you choose to live in a container home, a reality is that noise pollution may sometimes contaminate the space. Similarly, in the photo below, you can see how the decision was made to use bunk beds in a living area to use space that was available towards the ceiling. The lower bunk, with a cushion behind it, is able to be used as both an afternoon sitting area as well as a bed when it's time to go to sleep.

Interior Design Option 4: Fold Out Table

A fold out table is a fabulous way to design a kitchen area in a container home because it gives the home greater utility and versatility. It also allows more square footage to exist in the house when dinner isn't being served. A container home can always use more space, and a fold out table provides just that.

Additionally, in the photo below, the table is attached to a dresser of sorts. The china on the dresser along with books and a speaker suggest that this shelving unit is used for both the bedroom and the eatery. This type of shelving unit, with openings on either end of it, also serves to provide more space to the entire area of the home.

Lastly, take note of the drawers beneath the bed. On top of the drawers is a bench that can be used as a place to sit while eating. While you would still need to use collapsible chairs at the opposite end of the table if you were dining with more than a couple of people, the multidimensional ability of this drawer/bench combination offers a simplified design tactic.

Interior Design Option 5: From Table to Framed Photo

In addition to simply folding a table and letting the legs of the table be exposed on the wall, you can opt to design or buy a collapsible table that has a photo or painting on its underside. In the example provided, the table legs are cut in a way that allows them to be used as a frame when they are folded and on the wall. This is an even more innovative way to hide your table when it's not being used. When you invite an individual into your home, this idea is sure to be one that will attract some comments.

Chapter 8: How to Give Your Home an Addition

Step 1: Check Your Permits

Chapter 5 provided a better understanding of the initial permits and codes that your shipping container home must meet in order for it to meet state regulations and standards; however, you must go back and review your codes and permits when you consider building an addition to your shipping container home because you need to make sure that the type of addition that you seek to build won't put the integrity and stability of your home into jeopardy.

Step 2: Have a Design Ready

By this point, I think that it may sound redundant, but it's important to have your addition mapped out before you actually build it. There were situations where a shipping container homeowner thought that he or she could begin adding onto a home without properly laying it out dimensionally on paper first. While the goal was to build a home that was larger than previously, the result ended up being wasted materials, time, money, and energy. Don't let this happen to you. Design your addition before building it, and seek out external help if necessary.

Step 3: Pick an Area of Your House that is the Least-Used

Let's say that you currently own a lovely forty-foot shipping container home and you're looking to expand it. Let's say you have a baby on the way, and you know that your current living situation is simply not going to offer enough room after the baby arrives. When you're initially designing the plans for your addition, it's important to try and add on to the home in a location that makes the most sense and disturbs the current details of your home in the smallest ways possible. For example, while you may think that the bathroom will be the best area of the house to knock down and rebuild because of its small size, this is probably not the case. Think of your plumbing costs. If you knock out the bathroom and rebuild it in a different area of the house, you're going to have to pay someone again to install the plumbing fixtures. Due to factors such as these, choose an area of the house that is not being used in a crucial way.

Along these same lines, it's okay if your shipping container home is an obscure shape once the addition is built, because with these homes it sometimes seems like the funkier the aesthetic, the better. If the wall in your living room area is only used for hanging pictures and watching television, you could knock out that large wall and attach an additional shipping container to it. A good rule of thumb is to be innovative when designing your addition, and change as little as possible when implementing the addition.

Step 4: Set Clear Priorities

If the giant bay window in your home is an area of the house that you love, find a way to keep it. Just because a window would be the easiest area of the house to add an addition to, if this part of your home is something you don't want to live without, then don't make that compromise. Find a way to fit it all into your overall plan. If it all simply cannot be kept, this fact will reveal itself in time and you can alter your plans.

Step 5: Consider Connecting Containers via Doorway

While setting the foundation for an addition to your shipping container home will require knowledge of how to lay down cement and you may need a contractor to make this happen, designing how your shipping containers will connect to one another doesn't need to be complicated. Instead of cutting the steel of your current unit to match the wide area of the door opening that exists on the new shipping container, consider connecting your two units in a way that utilizes only a small door cut.

If you plan your design so that the new unit that you're adding simply facilitates more bedroom space or a workshop area, you won't need to cut a giant hole in one or both of your shipping container units. You will only have to cut a hole that fits the size of a doorway. This will save you time as well as the potential need to hire a professional to make this cut for you.

Chapter 9: How to Be a Handyman, Providing Maintenance for Your Container

Even though building or owning a shipping container home is cheaper than subscribing to pay a mortgage for thirty-plus years of your life, it's still no small drop in the bucket. A shipping container home is an investment, and your container needs to be taken care of to ensure that it has the longest life possible. This chapter will focus on steps that you can take to lengthen the life of your shipping container. The last thing that any new homeowner wants, shipping container or standard two-story home, is to purchase something only for it to deteriorate and falter under environmental and other types of pressure. This chapter will focus on what you can do as a responsible homeowner to reduce the wear and tear of your home over time. With these tactics in use, you'll greatly increase the overall and long term value of your home.

Tactic 1: External Cladding

You can think of external cladding to be the equivalent of a protective layer similar to a skin or coating. This will protect the outside of your home from weather and other factors that will wear it down over time. Cladding does not remove the original steel exterior of the shipping container home, but instead pads it. Additionally, external cladding can serve to make the steel quality of your home appear less industrial and softer. The types of cladding that you can purchase to both weatherproof and improve the outer look of your home include:

- Stone cladding
- Timber cladding
- Weatherboard cladding
- Brick cladding
- Fiber Cement cladding

Adding external cladding to your home will ensure that termites and rot cannot get to it. External cladding can last well over fifty years. You can find cladding for as little as $3.00 per piece to as much as $30.00 per piece. The vast range in price can give you many possibilities and choices.

Tactic 2: Treat Areas of Rust as Quickly as Possible

We have already briefly discussed how rust can damage the overall quality of a shipping container home, so it should be no surprise that if you treat areas of rust as quickly as possible, you can avoid having to make pricey decisions for your home at a later time. While it's possible to remove rust using ingredients from your home, such as lemon, this method is not advisable to be used on something as valuable as your container house. Instead, try the following combination of products if you want to see maximum results against any rust that has accumulated:

- 7 cups lime-free glycerin
- 1 cup sodium citrate. This product can be found at the drugstore
- 6 cups lukewarm water
- Powdered calcium carbonate (also known as chalk).

Keep adding chalk as needed until a paste forms. After you have your pasty mixture, spread the paste over the rust-stained area with a spreading tool of your choice and leave it there until it hardens. Once hard, use a metal tool, like a chisel or prong, to scrape away the residue from the mixture that you have made. This should remove the rust that was once on the house, but if it doesn't, repeat this process until it's gone. Remember, as a container homeowner, you should be looking for rust on a regular basis, because this is one of the problems that frequently occurs on these types of homes.

Additionally, it's important to realize that when the shipping container is transported to you, it's likely that there will be dents in the roof because of how shipping of these units usually occurs. Be sure to get the dents out of your roof when you start building you first start building you home. This will save you trouble in the future.

Tactic 3: Use Corrosion Resistant Paint

Another method that can serve as a form of maintenance for your container home is to apply corrosion-resistant paint to your unit. If you use this method of protection, consider using it when your home is first being built so that you can prevent future corrosion. You can use this type of paint after an area of your unit has already started to rust, but this is less of a preventative measure before the incident and more of an attempt to fix something after it has already occurred. Take the time to use the precaution of corrosion resistant paint when your home is first built so that you can avoid the pain that rust brings to the eye when you see it on your shiny new living space.

Tactic 4: Grease

Another tactic that seems to be more preventative is to use grease in areas that are prone to sticking or rusting over time. These areas include the door hinges of the shipping container unit (if you decide to keep them), window jams, and door handles.

Because shipping containers last decades being transported internationally and overseas, we know that they are relatively long lasting and durable; however, because people have not been using them as homes for very long, it's hard to know exactly how long they last and what their great limitations seem to be. Of course, the most current and significant limitation in terms of maintenance seems to be rust. The accumulation of rust should be avoided whenever possible. When rust does occur, the solvent that was presented in this chapter will definitely help to eliminate what rust has collected. As with any type of injury, if a significant problem can be avoided by small and frequent measures, performing these measures is the preferable option in order to avoid a large problem in the future.

Resources

While I certainly hope that the information presented in this book has given you a good foundation from which to start your shipping container home project, there are countless other resources, some of which I would like to share with you. My hope is that these additional resources will help you gain even more information for all of your shipping container needs.

- **www.containerhomeplans.org** is a great online starting point for everything related to building a container home. If you subscribe to their mailing list, they will give you four free chapters of their own e-book, titled *How to Build a Shipping Container Home: The Complete Guide!*

- **www.diychatroom.com** offers an exclusive forum for aspiring shipping container homeowners. You can chat with other people who are in similar positions as you, and find advice through a more conversational avenue.

- Another audio resource that might be helpful if you love podcasts is to tune into a podcast called Tiny House Chat. While not exclusively dedicated to shipping container homes, this podcast can offer design options for smaller spaces and more details on how your home should be properly constructed.

- **trybuild.org.au** is an Australian site that focuses on training socially disadvantaged unemployed people to gain the necessary life skills needed to build a container home.

Conclusion

Thanks again for taking the time to buy my book **Shipping Container Homes.**

You should now have a good understanding of the process of how to build a shipping container home.

If you enjoyed this book, please take the time to leave me a review on Amazon. I appreciate your honest feedback, and it really helps me to continue producing high quality books.

Simply type out the link below in your browser:
http://amzn.to/2dvj3C1

Other books by this Author

Beekeeping: Create your own backyard beehive colony and make delicious organic honey **http://amzn.to/2dugsmP**

Made in the USA
Middletown, DE
04 June 2020